CHECKERBOARD SOCIAL STUDIES LIBRARY

DEFENDING THE NATION

Defending the Nation

THE

FBI

John Hamilton
ABDO Publishing Company

visit us at
www.abdopublishing.com

Published by ABDO Publishing Company, 4940 Viking Drive, Edina, Minnesota 55435.
Copyright © 2007 by Abdo Consulting Group, Inc. International copyrights reserved in all
countries. No part of this book may be reproduced in any form without written permission from
the publisher. The Checkerboard Library™ is a trademark and logo of ABDO Publishing
Company.

Printed in the United States.

Cover Photos: front cover, Corbis; back cover, U.S. Air Force
Interior Photos: Corbis pp. 1, 5, 8, 11, 14, 16-17, 18, 20, 21, 22, 24, 25, 28; Getty Images pp. 9,
    11, 13, 17, 22-23, 26-27

Series Coordinator: Megan M. Gunderson
Editors: Rochelle Baltzer, Megan M. Gunderson
Art Direction & Cover Design: Neil Klinepier

Library of Congress Cataloging-in-Publication Data

Hamilton, John, 1959-
   The Federal Bureau of Investigation / John Hamilton.
      p. cm. -- (Defending the nation)
   Includes bibliographical references and index.
   ISBN-13: 978-1-59679-757-4
   ISBN-10: 1-59679-757-6 (alk. paper)
   1. United States. Federal Bureau of Investigation--Juvenile literature. 2. Criminal investigation--
United States--Juvenile literature. I. Title II. Series: Hamilton, John, 1959- . Defending the
nation.

   HV8144.F43H36 2007
   363.250973--dc22

                                                                            2005035543

Contents

The Federal Bureau of Investigation

The Federal Bureau of Investigation (FBI) is the main investigative force of the U.S. government. More specifically, the FBI investigates federal crimes for the U.S. Department of Justice (DOJ). The DOJ makes sure laws are obeyed and crimes are prevented.

The U.S. Congress makes laws. When someone breaks a law, he or she has committed a crime. The FBI investigates the most serious crimes carried out in the United States and brings lawbreakers to justice. It works for the safety and security of all U.S. citizens.

Today, preventing **terrorism** is one of the FBI's biggest jobs. The FBI also collects information about other groups and individuals that might be dangerous. This is called intelligence gathering.

The head of the FBI is called the director. He or she is appointed by the president and approved by the U.S. Senate. The director guides the FBI from its headquarters in Washington, D.C. Today, the FBI has 56 field offices in major U.S cities. It also has more than 400 offices in smaller U.S. cities and more than 50 international offices.

FBI headquarters has been in the J. Edgar Hoover FBI Building in Washington, D.C., since the mid-1970s.

Timeline

1908 - Attorney General Charles J. Bonaparte formed the Bureau of Investigation; Stanley W. Finch was named its first director.

1932 - The Bureau of Investigation became the U.S. Bureau of Investigation; the bureau founded its crime lab.

1935 - The U.S. Bureau of Investigation became known as the Federal Bureau of Investigation.

1951 - After an FBI investigation, Julius and Ethel Rosenberg were convicted of passing secret information to the Soviets.

1975 - A U.S. Senate investigation found the FBI guilty of spying illegally on U.S. citizens and committing burglaries to obtain information.

1999 - The FBI began using the Integrated Automated Fingerprint Identification System.

2001 - On September 11, terrorists attacked the United States, which led to the FBI's increased focus on counterterrorism.

2004 - The U.S. Congress passed the Intelligence Reform and Terrorism Prevention Act.

2005 - The National Security Branch was established.

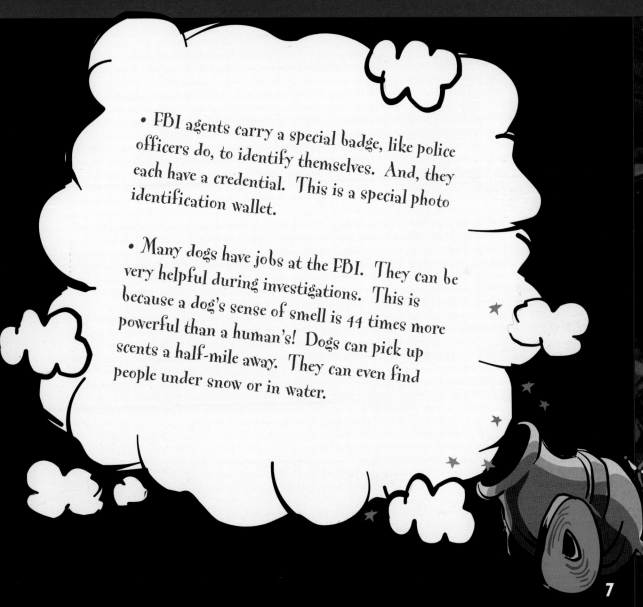

- FBI agents carry a special badge, like police officers do, to identify themselves. And, they each have a credential. This is a special photo identification wallet.

- Many dogs have jobs at the FBI. They can be very helpful during investigations. This is because a dog's sense of smell is 44 times more powerful than a human's! Dogs can pick up scents a half-mile away. They can even find people under snow or in water.

Attorney General Charles J. Bonaparte

The FBI traces its roots to 1908. That year, Attorney General Charles J. Bonaparte formed a special police force to examine federal crimes. This new investigative team became the Bureau of Investigation. It worked within the DOJ.

Today, these investigators are known as special agents. Bonaparte appointed the first special agents to work in the Bureau of Investigation. He also made Stanley W. Finch the first director of the bureau.

In 1932, the organization's name changed to the U.S. Bureau of Investigation. And in 1935, the name changed again. This time it became the Federal Bureau of Investigation, the name we use today.

At first, FBI special agents investigated cases such as illegal land sales. They also investigated cases such as car thefts that

WANTED

JOHN HERBERT DILLINGER

On June 23, 1934, HOMER S. CUMMINGS, Attorney General of the United States, under the authority vested in him by an Act of Congress approved June 6, 1934, offered a reward of

$10,000.00
for the capture of John Herbert Dillinger or a reward of

$5,000.00
for information leading to the arrest of John Herbert Dillinger.

DESCRIPTION

Age, 32 years; Height, 5 feet 7-1/8 inches; Weight, 153 pounds; Build, medium; Hair, medium chestnut; Eyes, grey; Complexion, medium; Occupation, machinist; Marks and scars, 1/2 inch scar back left hand, scar middle upper lip, brown mole between eyebrows.

As to any of the aforesaid rewards and all questions and disputes that may arise among claimants to the foregoing rewards shall be final and conclusive. The right is reserved to distribute portions of any of said rewards as between several claimants. No aforesaid rewards shall be paid to any official or employee of the Department.

If in possession of any information concerning the whereabouts of John Dillinger, communicate immediately by telephone or telegraph collect to the nearest office of the Division of Investigation, United States Department of Justice, addresses of which are set forth on the reverse side of this notice.

JOHN EDGAR HOOVER, DIRECTOR,
DIVISION OF INVESTIGATION,
UNITED STATES DEPARTMENT OF JUSTICE,
WASHINGTON, D. C.

involved crossing state lines. But during the 1930s, crime waves swept the United States. Kidnappings, bank robberies, and other violent crimes were on the rise. So, Congress increased the FBI's authority to investigate these serious crimes.

The FBI helped train local and state police in its investigative methods. And, FBI agents began tracking criminals on their own. They hunted down famous gangsters, such as John Dillinger and George "Machine Gun" Kelly. Kelly is credited with inventing the term "G-Men." This nickname for special agents is short for Government Men.

In 1932, the FBI began publishing a list of most wanted fugitives. In 1950, this became the Ten Most Wanted Fugitives Program. Today, the FBI also maintains a list of most wanted terrorists. And just like in its early days, the FBI offers rewards for information leading to the arrest of major criminals.

During **World War II**, the FBI broke up groups of German spies. These foreign spies had tried to commit **sabotage** against the United States. After World War II, the United States and the Soviet Union entered the **Cold War**. And with this, the threat of spies continued.

One of the FBI's main focuses during the Cold War was on arresting **communist** spies. Many of these spies were accused of stealing military secrets, such as plans for **nuclear** weapons. The most famous people arrested by the FBI for this crime were Julius and Ethel Rosenberg. In 1951, they were convicted of passing secret information to the Soviets.

During the 1960s and 1970s, many groups spoke out against the **Vietnam War**. Others promoted **civil rights**. The FBI investigated these protest groups. But a 1975 U.S. Senate investigation found that the FBI had broken laws. Agents had illegally spied on U.S. citizens and committed burglaries during some of their investigations. So, the DOJ created new guidelines to stop this **abuse**.

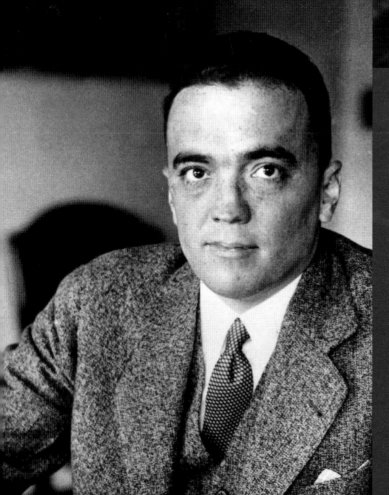

J. Edgar Hoover

Lawyer J. Edgar Hoover began working in the DOJ in 1917. In 1924, he became the director of the FBI. He led the FBI for 48 years, until his death in 1972.

When Hoover took over the FBI, the bureau was struggling. Hoover reorganized it and publicized its successful investigations. Hoover and his G-Men gained fame for tracking down criminals such as John Dillinger, Pretty Boy Floyd, and Baby Face Nelson. And in 1950, he started the still-successful Ten Most Wanted Fugitives Program.

Despite his successes, Hoover was often criticized for abusing his power as director of the FBI. During his years as director, some politicians and private citizens even had information illegally used against them. In 1968, Congress passed a law limiting FBI directors after Hoover to a ten-year term.

John Dillinger

Baby Face Nelson

Pretty Boy Floyd

Crimes the FBI Investigates

When the FBI began in 1908, its mission fit the crimes of that time period. For example, cars became popular in the first part of the 1900s. To avoid getting caught by local police, criminals began driving stolen cars to other states. In response, the bureau started investigating crimes such as these that involved crossing state borders.

As time went by, advancements in technology created new opportunities for criminals. The FBI's responsibilities grew to fight these threats. Today, the FBI investigates more than 350 violations of the law. Most of these crimes fall into seven broad categories.

One of these categories is **counterterrorism**. Terrorists can be extremely hard to find. But after the terrorist attacks on September 11, 2001, the FBI put more focus on this category. The FBI greatly increased its ability to counter, or work against, terrorists and stop them before they strike. Today, the FBI works closely with police and other government agencies to defeat terrorism.

Many countries use spies to gather intelligence about foreign governments. The FBI works to stop spies inside the United States from stealing government or military secrets. FBI agents especially focus on preventing the theft of weapons of mass destruction. These include **nuclear** bombs and equipment used in **germ warfare**. These tasks are all part of the foreign counterintelligence category.

The FBI investigates many kinds of terrorism. After the September 11 attacks, FBI agents helped investigate the use of chemicals as weapons.

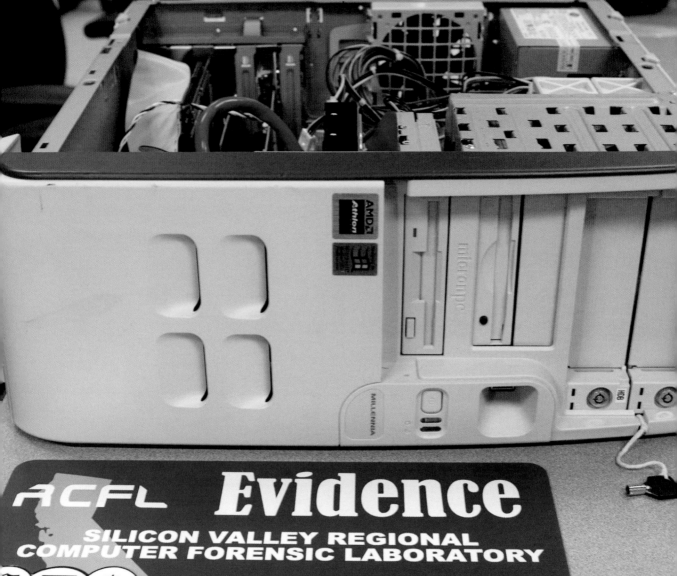

Violent crime is another main investigative category at the FBI. It includes gang violence, kidnapping, and crimes against children. So when people are threatened or killed, the FBI is often called upon to help local police.

Sometimes, groups of people band together to commit crimes. These crimes are hard to stop because the groups are secretive and powerful. And, their crimes are well planned. Crimes committed by organized groups can be violent and destructive. These activities fall under the FBI's organized crime category.

To fight organized crime, the FBI targets entire organizations, rather than individual crimes. Sometimes, FBI agents even work undercover to gather information. They disguise themselves as members of a group in order to catch criminals.

The FBI also investigates people who use computers and the Internet to commit crimes. These cybercriminals may steal from or harm citizens and businesses. Foreign countries may also attack U.S. government and military computer networks. So, the FBI's cybercrime experts actively investigate and prevent these damaging attacks.

FBI investigators often collect a cybercriminal's computer as evidence. The FBI works with the Silicon Valley Regional Computer Forensics Laboratory to investigate criminal computer activities, such as Internet crime.

Some crimes are nonviolent. Frequently, these crimes are related to illegal business practices. They often fall into the white-collar crime category. "White collar" refers to the white shirt often worn by businesspeople.

Sometimes, businesspeople **abuse** their power and cheat others. They may deceive banks, insurance companies, or other businesses to steal money. White-collar criminals may also illegally harm the **environment**. Or, they may trick people into giving up money or property over the telephone.

All U.S. citizens have certain rights and freedoms no matter their race or religion. Crimes related to equality and political and social freedom fall under the **civil rights** category. Within this category, the FBI investigates **hate crimes**. It also investigates cases of police **brutality** and voting and housing **discrimination**.

White-collar crime can involve stealing secret information, such as in identity theft cases. This is when someone steals personal information, including credit card numbers or bank account details.

The FBI also investigates cases that involve stealing trade secrets from one business and giving them to another.

At the FBI, those who decode information leading to arrests are just as important as those who make the arrests.

The FBI has two kinds of jobs. They are special agents and support employees. Special agents have the authority to enforce certain U.S. government laws. They investigate crimes, arrest criminals, carry firearms, and sometimes work undercover.

In movies and on television, the job of a special agent can seem glamorous, dangerous, and exciting. It can be all these things! But in reality, special agents also spend time interviewing people, testifying in federal court, and writing reports. FBI special agents must be persistent and committed to all aspects of their jobs to bring criminals to justice.

It takes people with many different skills to run such a large, complicated organization. A very important part of the FBI's mission is to gather intelligence, or information. Support jobs include language specialists who translate foreign intelligence into English. The FBI has specialists who can speak almost any language.

Other important support jobs at the FBI include computer programmers, laboratory scientists, and lawyers. The FBI also employs cryptanalysts who decode secret messages. And, it hires engineers, pilots, nurses, writers, and secretaries. People with a variety of skills serve their country by working for the FBI.

Special Agent Training

The FBI Academy is one of the world's finest law enforcement training centers.

Each year, thousands of people apply to become FBI special agents. Special agent candidates must be between 23 and 36 years old. They must be in great physical shape and be a U.S. citizen. Candidates need to have a college degree. And, at least three years of professional work experience is often required.

About one in 20 people who apply are accepted for FBI training. Recruits receive 17 weeks of **intense** training at the FBI Academy in Quantico, Virginia. There, they attend law and science classes. They also learn how to conduct criminal investigations.

As part of their schooling, future agents learn self-defense skills such as martial arts. They also learn to shoot different kinds of firearms. And, they learn how to clean their weapons and shoot at targets. Agents must be able to make split-second judgments when lives are at risk. Being an FBI special agent can be both stressful and rewarding.

After graduating from the academy, recruits receive their credentials. These documents prove that they are now FBI special agents. As they progress in their careers, agents are required to stay in good physical condition. And, they are tested on firearms handling four times each year.

Training at the FBI Academy is demanding and realistic. Special agent recruits make regular use of a pretend town called Hogan's Alley. It includes many buildings, such as a bank, a post office, and a drugstore.

In Hogan's Alley, professional actors play the parts of the townspeople. There, FBI instructors send recruits on training missions that simulate real-life situations. By working with the actors, recruits can practice investigative methods. They learn how to interview witnesses and confront dangerous situations.

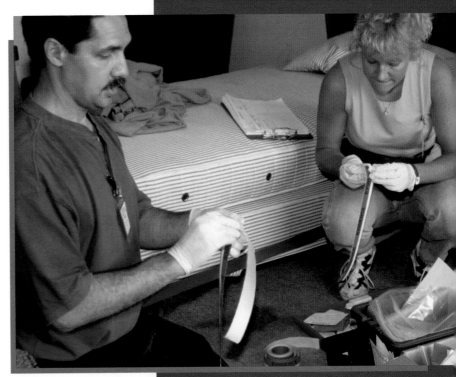

The FBI Laboratory

To successfully investigate a crime, the FBI must often collect and **analyze** physical evidence. Evidence that is properly analyzed and identified can be used to prove who committed a crime. A weapon, a fiber from someone's clothing, or even a tiny drop of blood can be used as evidence.

At a crime scene, the FBI is careful to collect even the smallest bits of evidence. The evidence is then sent to the FBI Laboratory. The FBI Laboratory is housed within the J. Edgar Hoover FBI Building in Washington, D.C.

In order to improve its criminal investigations, the FBI has been running a crime laboratory since 1932. There, highly trained scientists examine evidence.

Following a crime, scientists search for trace evidence. This type of evidence, such as hair or fibers, may be left behind by a suspect or a criminal.

Evidence collection is a vital part of a criminal investigation.

The FBI Laboratory uses the most advanced scientific instruments available. And, the laboratory examines more than 1 million pieces of evidence each year!

Fingerprints are common pieces of evidence collected at crime scenes. Sweat and oil on our skin make a mark on everything we touch. This means faint fingerprint patterns are left behind on objects. These patterns can be detected with special equipment.

Each person's fingerprints are unique. This means no two people have the same set of prints. So, fingerprints can be used for identification. Finding a person's unique fingerprints can prove that he or she was at a crime scene.

In July 1999, the FBI began using a computerized system to store criminal histories and fingerprints. This new system is called the Integrated Automated Fingerprint Identification System. It increases the speed with which fingerprints can be matched to criminals. And, it helps the FBI share criminal histories and fingerprints with other law enforcement agencies.

The FBI has more than 250 million fingerprint records on file. And, it receives 37,000 new records each day!

In addition to fingerprints, the FBI tests DNA. DNA exists in the cells of our bodies. Just like fingerprints, every person's DNA is unique. FBI scientists can trace a person's DNA from evidence such as blood, skin, or hair. And like fingerprints, DNA evidence can prove someone was at a crime scene.

In addition to laboratory tests, FBI investigators commonly use polygraphs. Polygraph machines are also called lie detectors. These machines detect tiny changes in a person's blood pressure, breathing, or sweating. A person cannot easily control these small changes. So, the changes give investigators a good idea about whether a person is lying.

Another powerful tool the FBI uses is criminal profiling. By carefully examining a crime scene, investigators can make a good guess about a criminal's characteristics. Determining a criminal's personality, age, gender, and motive for committing a crime can greatly help law enforcement. These elements help narrow down the list of possible suspects.

DNA analysis has been used as criminal evidence in the United States since 1986. A national database called the Combined DNA Index System (CODIS) allows investigators to compare new DNA evidence with DNA samples already on file.

Today, one of the FBI's main missions is to protect and defend the United States against **terrorist** threats. The U.S. government wanted to find out who was behind the September 11 attacks. So, the FBI launched its largest investigation in history. It identified many possible terrorists in an effort to prevent future attacks.

Despite this effort, the FBI was criticized for not doing enough to prevent the September 11 **terrorist** attacks. So in 2002, Director Robert S. Mueller III reorganized the FBI. He hired hundreds of additional agents to investigate terrorist threats. Now, the bureau has an increased focus on stopping terrorism.

In 2004, the U.S. Congress passed the Intelligence Reform and Terrorism Prevention Act. This act affected the FBI. There is still a director of the FBI. But now, there is also a director of national intelligence. He or she oversees the information gathering of several government agencies, including the FBI.

Today, the FBI cooperates and shares intelligence with other government and law enforcement agencies. This includes the Central Intelligence Agency. And in 2005, the FBI established the National Security Branch (NSB). The NSB coordinates the FBI's counterterrorism and counterintelligence efforts.

These developments have increased the FBI's role as one of the world's best investigators of criminal activity. The FBI will continue to work hard to keep Americans safe from harm.

Mueller became director of the FBI just one week before September 11. After the attacks, the FBI reorganized its priorities, with terrorism prevention at the top of the list.

Glossary

abuse - to use incorrectly or improperly.

analyze - to determine the meaning of something by breaking down its parts.

brutal - particularly severe, harmful, or cruel.

civil rights - the individual rights of a citizen, such as the right to vote or freedom of speech.

Cold War - a period of tension and hostility between the United States and its allies and the Soviet Union and its allies after World War II.

communism - a social and economic system in which everything is owned by the government and given to the people as needed.

discrimination - unfair treatment based on factors such as a person's race, religion, or gender.

environment - all the surroundings that affect the growth and well-being of a living thing.

germ warfare - the use of harmful organisms, such as bacteria, as weapons.

hate crime - a crime directed at a specific person or group, often based on race, religion, or gender.

intense - marked by great energy, determination, or concentration.

nuclear - of or relating to the energy created when atoms are divided or combined. An atomic bomb is a nuclear weapon.

sabotage (SA-buh-tahzh) - to damage or destroy something on purpose. Sabotage is often carried out by a person who wants to harm an enemy nation.

terrorism - the use of terror, violence, or threats to frighten people into action. A person who commits an act of terrorism is called a terrorist.

Vietnam War - from 1957 to 1975. A long, failed attempt by the United States to stop North Vietnam from taking over South Vietnam.

World War II - from 1939 to 1945, fought in Europe, Asia, and Africa. Great Britain, France, the United States, the Soviet Union, and their allies were on one side. Germany, Italy, Japan, and their allies were on the other side.

Web Sites

To learn more about the FBI, visit ABDO Publishing Company on the World Wide Web at **www.abdopublishing.com**. Web sites about the FBI are featured on our Book Links page. These links are routinely monitored and updated to provide the most current information available.

Index